DINOSAUR PROFILES

TYRANNOSAURUS

Titles in the Dinosaur Profiles series include:

DINOSAUR PROFILES

TYRANNOSAURUS

Text by Fabio Marco Dalla Vecchia
Illustrations by Leonello Calvetti and Luca Massini

BLACKBIRCH®
PRESS

THOMSON
★
GALE

San Diego • Detroit • New York • San Francisco • Cleveland • New Haven, Conn. • Waterville, Maine • London • Munich

For more information, contact
The Gale Group, Inc.
27500 Drake Rd.
Farmington Hills, MI 48331-3535
Or you can visit our Internet site at http://www.gale.com

Computer illustrations 3D and 2D: Leonello Calvetti and Luca Massini

Photographs: page 22 American Museum of Natural History, New York; page 23 (top) The Field Museum, Chicago; page 23 (bottom) Peter L. Larson/courtesy Black Hills Institute of Geological Research, Hill City

LIBRARY OF CONGRESS CATALOGING-IN-PUBLICATION DATA

Dalla Vecchia, Fabio Marco.
  Tyrannosaurus / text by Fabio Marco Dalla Vecchia; illustrations by Leonello Calvetti and Luca Massini.
      p. cm. — (Dinosaur profiles)
  Includes bibliographical references and index.
  ISBN 1-4103-0493-0 (paperback : alk. paper)
  ISBN 1-4103-0332-2 (hardback : alk. paper)
  1. Tyrannosaurus—Juvenile literature. I. Calvetti, Leonello. II. Massini, Luca. III. Title.
IV. Series: Dalla Vecchia, Fabio Marco. Dinosaur profiles.

  QE862.S3D43 2004
  567.912'9—dc22   2004008701

Printed in China
10 9 8 7 6 5 4 3 2

CONTENTS

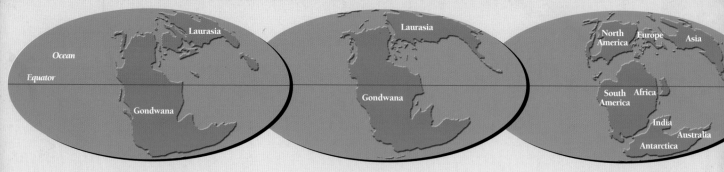

Late Triassic
227–206 million years ago

Early Jurassic
206–176 million years ago

Middle Jurassic
176–159 million years ago

A Changing World

Earth's long history began 4.6 billion years ago. Dinosaurs are some of the most fascinating animals from the planet's long past.

The word *dinosaur* comes from the word *dinosauria*. This word was invented by the English scientist Richard Owen in 1842. It comes from two Greek words, *deinos* and *sauros*. Together, these words mean "terrifying lizards."

The dinosaur era, also called the Mesozoic era, lasted from 248 million years ago to 65 million years ago. It is divided into three periods. The first, the Triassic period, lasted 42 million years. The second, the Jurassic period, lasted 61 million years. The third, the Cretaceous period, lasted 79 million years. Dinosaurs ruled the world for a huge time span of 160 million years.

Like dinosaurs, mammals appeared at the end of the Triassic period. During the time of dinosaurs, mammals were small animals the size of a mouse. Only after dinosaurs became extinct did mammals develop into the many forms that exist today. Humans never met Mesozoic dinosaurs. The dinosaurs were gone nearly 65 million years before humans appeared on Earth.

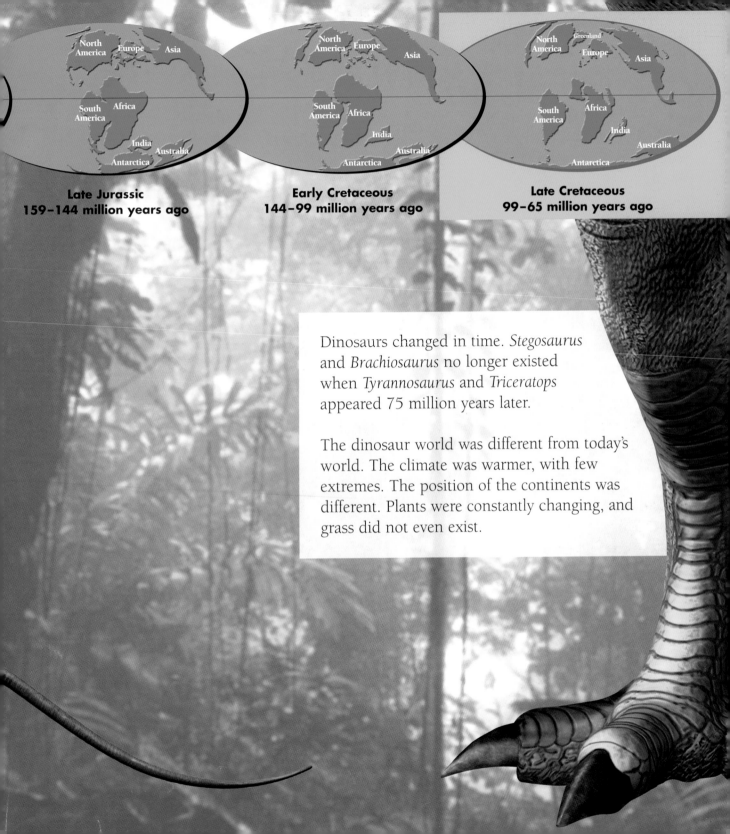

Late Jurassic
159–144 million years ago

Early Cretaceous
144–99 million years ago

Late Cretaceous
99–65 million years ago

Dinosaurs changed in time. *Stegosaurus* and *Brachiosaurus* no longer existed when *Tyrannosaurus* and *Triceratops* appeared 75 million years later.

The dinosaur world was different from today's world. The climate was warmer, with few extremes. The position of the continents was different. Plants were constantly changing, and grass did not even exist.

A Terrifying Giant

Tyrannosaurus rex was a saurischian dinosaur belonging to the group *Theropoda*, or theropods. It was the largest and fiercest predator of its time. The sight of an attacking *Tyrannosaurus rex* must have been terrifying.

An adult *Tyrannosaurus rex* (often shortened to *T.rex*) could grow to be as big as 42 feet (12.8 m) long and 13 feet (4 m) tall. It could weigh more than 7 tons (6 metric tons). Its huge head was about 5 feet (150 cm) long. Its powerful jaws had fifty-nine large, sharp, curved teeth that were 3 to 6 inches (8 to 16 cm) long and about an inch (2.5 cm) wide. Old, worn, and broken teeth were continuously replaced with new ones.

Despite its large body and head, *T.rex's* brain was only 11 inches (28 cm) long. Although the brain was small, the part related to smell was very well developed. *T.rex* used its excellent sense of smell to find distant prey and to recognize its mate during breeding season.

Sixty-five million years ago, *T.rex* lived on coastal plains near a shallow sea that divided North America in two. *T.rex* skeletons have been found in Alberta and Saskatchewan in Canada, and in Montana, North and South Dakota, Wyoming, Colorado, Texas, and New Mexico.

This map shows North America as it was in the Late Cretaceous period. The dark brown patches indicate mountains. The red dots indicate *Tyrannosaurus* fossil discovery sites.

NORTH

AMERICA

An adult *Tyrannosaurus* rex stood more than twice as tall as the average man.

Tyrannosaurus Babies

A mother *Tyrannosaurus* dug a low, circular nest in the mud. There, she laid long eggs with wrinkled shells. Because of her large size, she did not sit on the nest. Instead, the parents probably kept watch over the nest to protect the eggs and hatchlings. Small dinosaurs and large lizards would often prey upon helpless hatchlings.

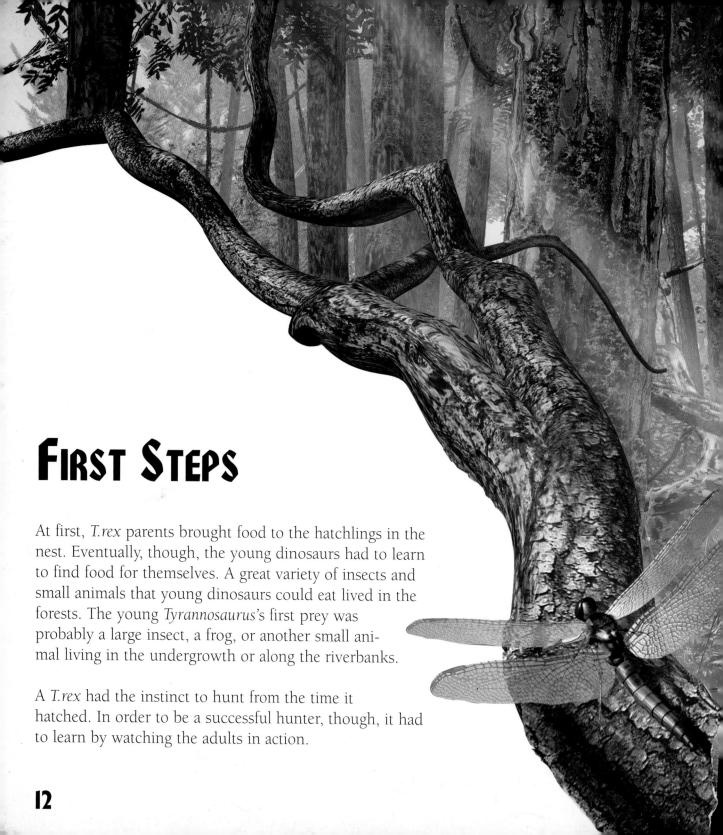

First Steps

At first, *T.rex* parents brought food to the hatchlings in the nest. Eventually, though, the young dinosaurs had to learn to find food for themselves. A great variety of insects and small animals that young dinosaurs could eat lived in the forests. The young *Tyrannosaurus*'s first prey was probably a large insect, a frog, or another small animal living in the undergrowth or along the riverbanks.

A *T.rex* had the instinct to hunt from the time it hatched. In order to be a successful hunter, though, it had to learn by watching the adults in action.

THE AMBUSH

Tyrannosaurus rex was the largest predator of its time. It was too big to run very fast. Luckily for *T.rex*, its favorite prey, the duck-billed *Edmontosaurus* and the bulky *Triceratops*, were not very fast either.

Instead of chasing its victims, *T.rex* hunted by ambushing its prey, which means to hide and surprise it. Hidden in the vegetation, *T.rex* waited for passing prey. It looked for the weakest, most helpless victims. These would be the young, the old, and the sick. *T.rex* would suddenly leap out and attack the defenseless victim. It would grip the prey with its jaws and shake its enormous head to tear away large shreds of flesh.

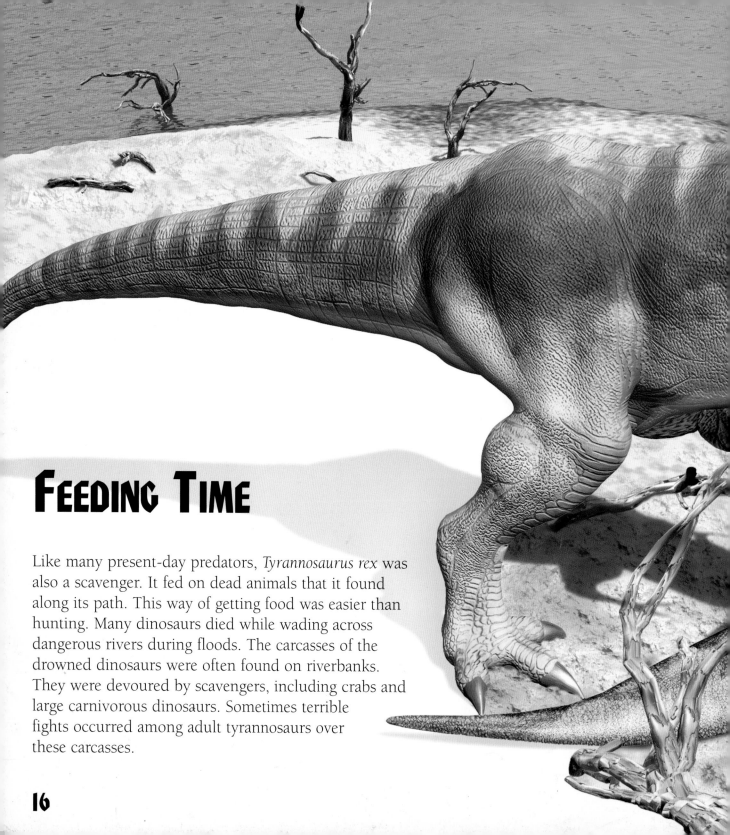

FEEDING TIME

Like many present-day predators, *Tyrannosaurus rex* was
also a scavenger. It fed on dead animals that it found
along its path. This way of getting food was easier than
hunting. Many dinosaurs died while wading across
dangerous rivers during floods. The carcasses of the
drowned dinosaurs were often found on riverbanks.
They were devoured by scavengers, including crabs and
large carnivorous dinosaurs. Sometimes terrible
fights occurred among adult tyrannosaurs over
these carcasses.

THE TYRANNOSAURUS BODY

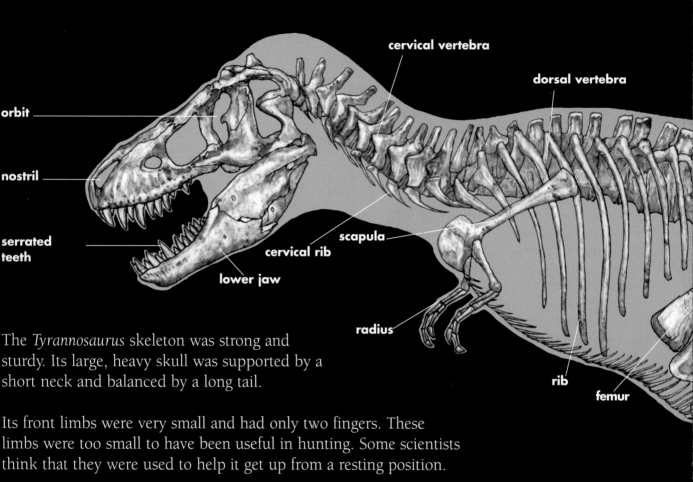

cervical vertebra

dorsal vertebra

orbit

nostril

serrated teeth

scapula

cervical rib

lower jaw

radius

rib

femur

The *Tyrannosaurus* skeleton was strong and sturdy. Its large, heavy skull was supported by a short neck and balanced by a long tail.

Its front limbs were very small and had only two fingers. These limbs were too small to have been useful in hunting. Some scientists think that they were used to help it get up from a resting position.

It had powerful legs. Each foot had three large toes with pointed claws and a smaller toe facing back and in. Like all predator dinosaurs, *T.rex* was a biped, meaning it walked on two legs. Some scientists have suggested that a *T.rex* could run 45 miles (72 km) per hour, but this estimate is too high for such a big dinosaur. *T.rex*, like all large terrestrial animals, was much slower. Its top speed was probably only 12.5 to 25 miles (20 to 40 km) per hour.

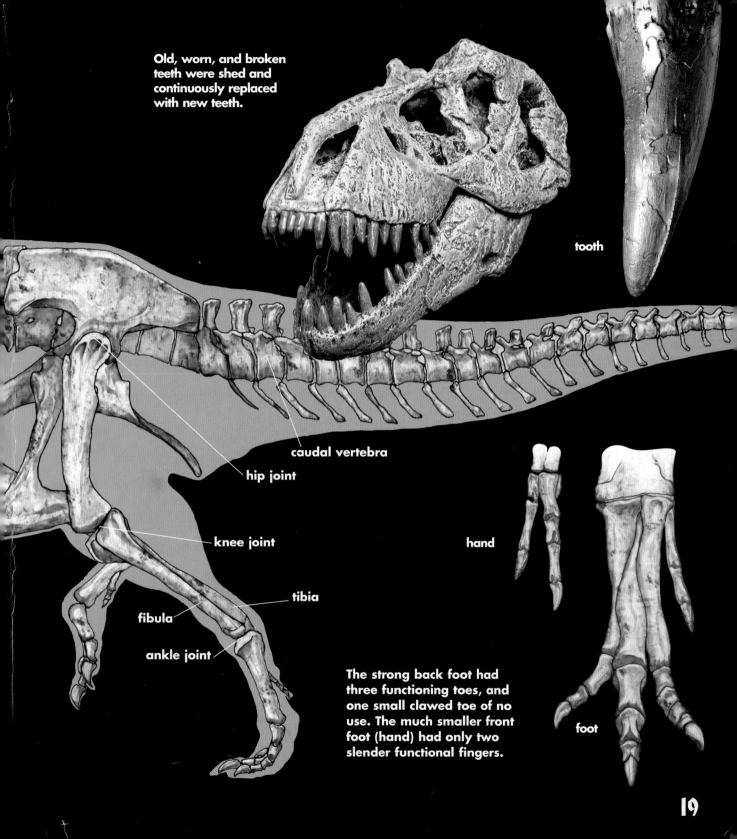

Old, worn, and broken teeth were shed and continuously replaced with new teeth.

tooth

caudal vertebra

hip joint

knee joint

tibia

fibula

ankle joint

hand

foot

The strong back foot had three functioning toes, and one small clawed toe of no use. The much smaller front foot (hand) had only two slender functional fingers.

Digging Up Tyrannosaurus

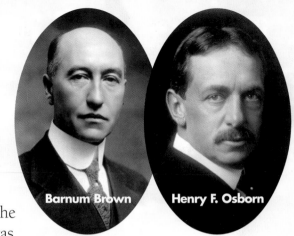

Barnum Brown   **Henry F. Osborn**

The first *Tyrannosaurus rex* skeleton was discovered in 1902 near Jordan, Montana, by paleontologist Barnum Brown. In 1905, paleontologist Henry F. Osborn named the fossil *Tyrannosaurus* (tyrant lizard) *rex* (king) because it was clearly a very large predator.

The fossil remains of tyrannosaurs are found in rocks formed by sediment in ancient rivers and lakes. Sometimes dinosaurs died near rivers. During floods, water carried the carcasses away and left them on the bottom of rivers or in flooded plains. While they were moved, the bodies were often broken apart. As a result, complete fossil skeletons of large dinosaurs are very rare.

Sediment settled on the remains of some dinosaurs, covering and protecting them from scavengers. After each flood, more layers of sediment piled up, eventually becoming solid rock. The slow movements of the earth's crust raised some beds of rock to form mountains and hills. Over time, wind and rain removed layers of rock. When the layer closest to the skeleton is removed, the dinosaur fossil can be seen.

Opposite, top: Sue is a nearly complete *T. rex* that is on display at the Field Museum in Chicago.

Opposite, below: Sue Hendrickson, who discovered Sue, is pictured here posing with the dinosaur's skull.

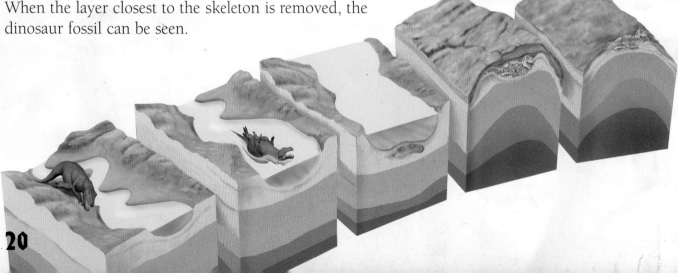

Dinosaur hunters usually give a nickname to the most complete skeletons. The discovery of a *Tyrannosaurus* nicknamed "Sue" caused a lot of excitement. Almost 90 percent of its original bones are preserved. Sue was named after Sue Hendrickson, who discovered it on a ranch in South Dakota. The skeleton was dug up and removed in 1990 by a commercial fossil collecting team.

The ranch where Sue was found turned out to be on a Sioux Indian reservation, however. The FBI took the bones away from the collecting team and stored them until the rightful owner could be determined. Eventually, a judge decided that Sue belonged to the rancher. The skeleton was

finally sold at a public auction in 1997. Sue was purchased for about $8.3 million by the Field Museum in Chicago, where it remains on display.

Other important *T.rex* skeletons are on display at the American Museum of Natural History in New York and at the Carnegie Museum in Pittsburgh. They are the first two *Tyrannosaurus* skeletons found by Barnum Brown in Montana. A young *T.rex* skeleton with the nickname "Tinker" is at the Cleveland Museum of Natural History in Ohio. New skeletons are often discovered.

Places where the fossils of the largest carnivorous dinosaurs have been found are noted on the map.

THE BIGGEST THEROPODS

Many scientists believe that the Chicxulub crater off the coast of Mexico was made by a meteorite that led to the extinction of the dinosaurs.

● *Spinosaurus*, northern Africa, 100–95 million years ago

● *Carcharodontosaurus*, northern Africa, 100–95 million years ago

● *Allosaurus*, USA, 155–148 million years ago

● *Giganotosaurus*, Argentina, 110–93 million years ago

Carnivorous dinosaurs as big or bigger than *Tyrannosaurus* have been discovered only recently. They all lived millions of years before *T.rex*. One such dinosaur was *Giganotosaurus*. *Giganotosaurus carolinii* was discovered in 1993 by Rubén Carolini in Argentina. *Giganotosaurus* was 42 feet (12.5 m) long and weighed 6.8 to 9 tons (6 to 8 metric tons). Its skull was 5.2 feet (1.53 m) long. Some say that *Giganotosaurus* was the largest theropod dinosaur, but others disagree.

Tyrannosaurus,
USA and Canada,
65 million years ago

THE GREAT EXTINCTION

Tyrannosaurus rex was one of the last dinosaurs. Sixty-five million years ago, all dinosaurs became extinct. This may have happened because a large meteorite struck Earth. A wide crater caused by a meteorite exactly 65 million years ago has been located along the coast of the Yucatán Peninsula in Mexico. The impact of the meteorite would have produced an enormous amount of dust. This dust would have stayed suspended in the atmosphere and blocked sunlight for a long time. A lack of sunlight would have caused a drastic drop of the earth's temperature and killed plants. The plant-eating dinosaurs would have died, starved and frozen. As a result, meat-eating dinosaurs would have had no prey and would also have starved.

Some scientists believe dinosaurs did not die out completely. They think that birds were feathered dinosaurs that survived the great extinction. That would make the present-day chicken and all of its feathered relatives descendants of the large dinosaurs.

The Evolution of Dinosaurs

The oldest dinosaur fossils are 220–225 million years old and have been found mainly in South America. They have also been found in Africa, India, and North America. Dinosaurs probably evolved from small and nimble bipedal reptiles like the Triassic *Lagosuchus* of Argentina. Dinosaurs were able to rule the world because their legs were held directly under the body, like those of modern mammals. This made them faster and less clumsy than other reptiles.

Triceratops is one of the Ornithischian dinosaurs, whose hip bones (inset) are shaped like those of modern birds.

Since 1887, dinosaurs have been divided into two groups based on the structure of their hips. Saurischian dinosaurs had hips shaped like those of modern lizards. Ornithischian dinosaurs had hips shaped like those of modern birds.

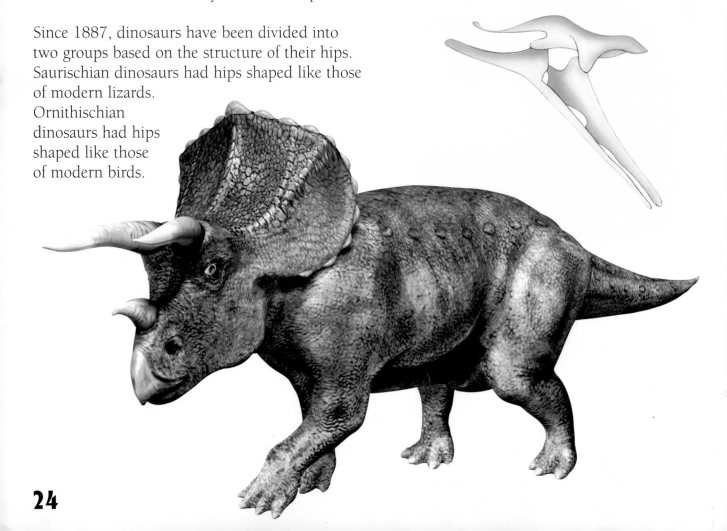

Tyrannosaurus is in the Saurischian group of dinosaurs, whose hip bones (inset) are shaped like those of modern lizards.

There are two main groups of saurischians. One group is sauropodomorphs. This group includes sauropods, such as *Brachiosaurus*. Sauropods ate plants and were quadrupedal, meaning they walked on four legs. The other group of saurischians, theropods, includes bipedal meat-eating predators. Some paleontologists believe birds are a branch of theropod dinosaurs.

Ornithischians are all plant eaters. They are divided into three groups. Thyreophorans include the quadrupedal stegosaurians, including *Stegosaurus*, and ankylosaurians, including *Ankylosaurus*. The other two groups are ornithopods, which includes *Edmontosaurus* and marginocephalians.

A Dinosaur's Family Tree

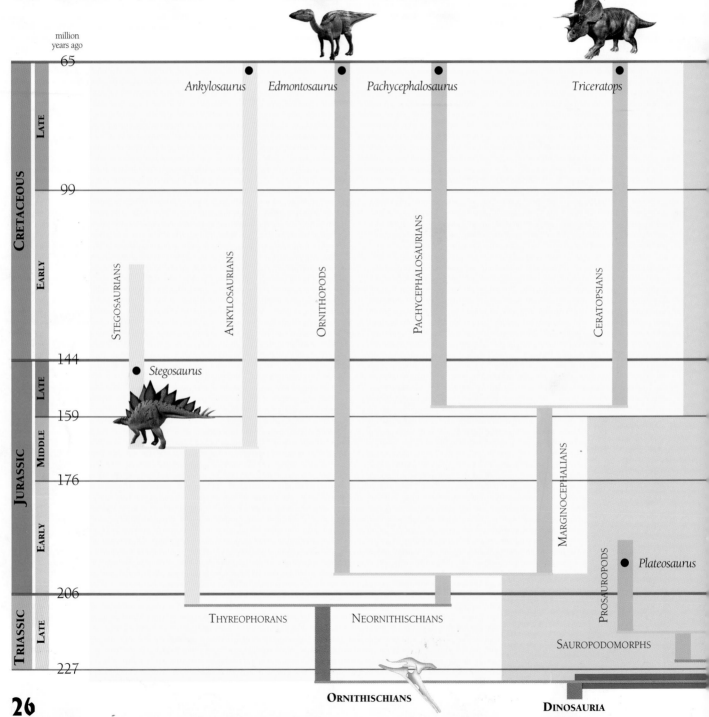

million years ago

65

CRETACEOUS

LATE

Ankylosaurus   *Edmontosaurus*   *Pachycephalosaurus*   *Triceratops*

99

EARLY

STEGOSAURIANS   ANKYLOSAURIANS   ORNITHOPODS   PACHYCEPHALOSAURIANS   CERATOPSIANS

144

JURASSIC

LATE

• *Stegosaurus*

159

MIDDLE

176

MARGINOCEPHALIANS

EARLY

• *Plateosaurus*

PROSAUROPODS

206

TRIASSIC

LATE

THYREOPHORANS   NEORNITHISCHIANS

SAUROPODOMORPHS

227

ORNITHISCHIANS   **DINOSAURIA**

SAUROPODS

Brachiosaurus

Scipionyx

ORNITHOLESTES

Ornithomimus

ORNITHOMIMOIDEANS

Tyrannosaurus

TYRANNOSAUROIDS

OVIRAPTOROSAURIANS

Caudipteryx

DEINONYCHOSAURIANS

Deinonychus

BIRDS

THEROPODSS

SAURISCHIANS

Glossary

Bipedal moving on two feet

Bone hard tissue made mainly of calcium phosphate

Carnivore meat eater

Caudal related to the tail

Cervical related to the neck

Claws sharp, pointed nails on the fingers and toes of predators

Cretaceous Period the period of geological time between 144 and 65 million years ago

Dorsal related to the back

Egg a large cell enclosed in a shell produced by reptiles and birds to reproduce themselves

Evolution changes in organisms over time

Femur thigh bone

Fibula the outer of the two bones in the lower leg

Fossil a part of an organism of an earlier geologic age, such as a skeleton or leaf imprint, that has been preserved in the earth's crust

Jurassic Period the period of geological time between 206 and 144 million years ago

Mesozoic Era the period of geological time between 248 and 65 million years ago

Meteorite a piece of iron or rock that falls to Earth from space

Orbit the opening in the skull surrounding the eye

Paleontologist a scientist who studies prehistoric life

Quadrupedal moving on four feet

Scapula shoulder blade

Scavenger animal that eats dead animals or plants

Sediment rock fragments and soil that settle on the bottom of a body of water

Skeleton the structure of an animal body, made up of bones

Skull the bones that form the cranium and the face

Terrestrial living on the land

Tibia the shinbone

Triassic Period the period of geological time between 248 and 206 million years ago

Vertebrae the bones of the backbone

For More Information

Books

Paul M. Barrett, *National Geographic Dinosaurs*.
Washington, DC: National Geographic Society, 2001.

Tim Haines, *Walking with Dinosaurs: A Natural History*.
New York: Dorling Kindersley, 2000.

David Lambert, Darren Naish, and Elizabeth Wyse,
*Dinosaur Encyclopedia: From Dinosaurs to the Dawn of
Man*. New York: Dorling Kindersley, 2001.

Web Sites

The Cyberspace Museum of Natural History
www.cyberspacemuseum.com/dinohall.html
An online dinosaur museum that includes descriptions and illustrations.

Dinodata
www.dinodata.net
A site that includes detailed descriptions of fossils,
illustrations, and news about dinosaur research and
recent discoveries.

**The Smithsonian National Museum of Natural
History**
www.nmnh.si.edu/paleo/dino
A virtual tour of the Smithsonian's National Museum
of Natural History dinosaur exhibits.

About the Author

Fabio Marco Dalla Vecchia is the curator of the Paleontological Museum of Monfalcone in Gorizia, Italy. He has participated in several paleontological field works in Italy and other countries and has directed paleontological excavations in Italy. He is the author of more than fifty scientific articles that have been published in national and international journals.

INDEX

Index